the truth about babies

Michael Stanford

ALLEN&UNWIN

First published in 2011

Allen & Unwin
Sydney, Melbourne, Auckland, London

83 Alexander Street
Crows Nest NSW 2065
Australia
Phone: (61 2) 8425 0100
Fax: (61 2) 9906 2218
Email: info@allenandunwin.com
Web: www.allenandunwin.com

Cataloguing-in-Publication details are available
from the National Library of Australia
www.trove.nla.gov.au

ISBN 978 1 74237 617 2

Internal design by saso content & design pty ltd
Set in 12/15 pt Aldus LT by saso content & design pty ltd
Printed in Australia by Ligare Pty Ltd, Sydney

10 9 8 7 6 5 4 3 2 1

PEFC™
PEFC/21-31-17

Introduction

No matter how much you prepare, how much you read or how much you listen to those who know more (or those who think they know more), babies are the ultimate surprise package. Once you leave the hospital, the flowers die and the cards stop, you are left with a job that is supposed to be natural and instinctive, yet in truth feels anything but. Babies can be often confusing, occasionally absurd, randomly moving, breathtakingly beautiful and, on a couple of instances, downright terrifying. No matter how involved I was as a dad, my wife shouldered most of the work (usually on the least amount of sleep). So this is really a dedication to the limitless efforts of those who care, love, cherish, worship and clean up after these tiny humans; from the ups and downs of emotions you never knew you had, to the ebb and flow of bodily fluids in colours you never thought possible. This book is also a tribute to babies themselves; how they bravely manage and cope with a world they seem utterly unprepared for. I would like to thank my generous friends who allowed me to use some very personal photos of their babies. Special thanks to Camilla and Rob, Robbie and Helene, and of course my beautiful wife, who will always deserve more credit than I ever will.

You sometimes wonder whether
your child is destined for greatness,

or a life in skateparks drinking
from brown paper bags.

The truth is you have no idea what is in store.

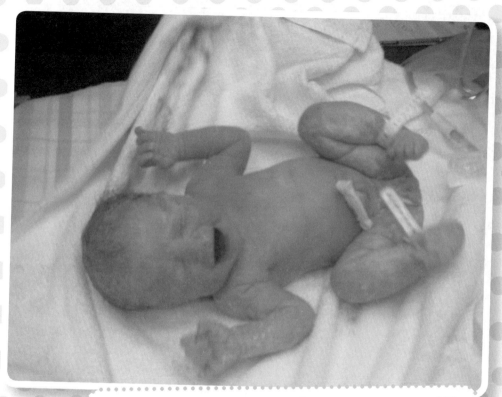

You do know their first scream will not be their last (however it will be the last that fills you with joy).

A baby will bring a family together
(even one best kept apart).

They will be smaller
than you imagined . . .

. . . much smaller,

and look more prepared for the English Channel than a maternity ward.

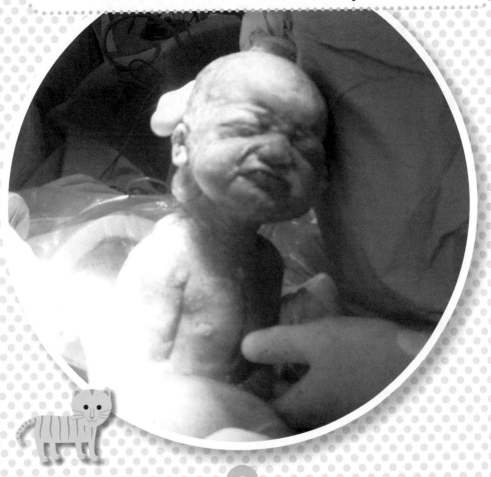

People will be a lot more interested in your baby than they were ever interested in you.

A baby will open your eyes to things you never thought possible,

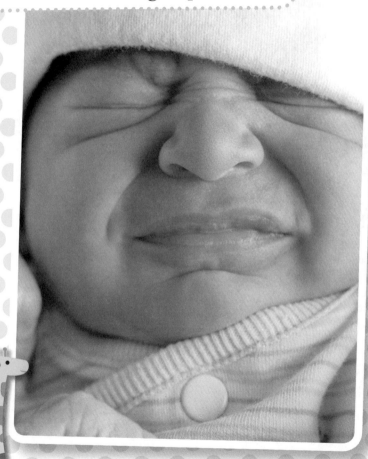

that something could
be so beautiful,

so loved,

so serious,

so curious,

or so like you.

A baby will teach you that sleep
does not necessarily follow a yawn,

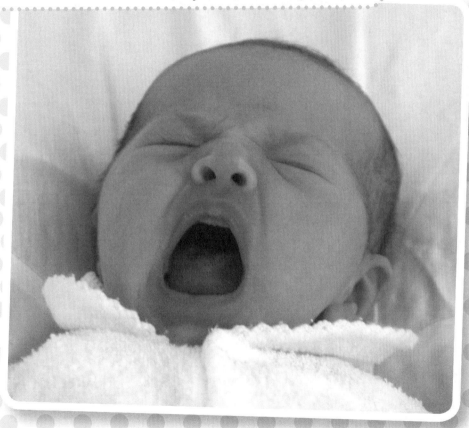

that a bath can get warmer,

that a poo requires the use of every muscle in their body,

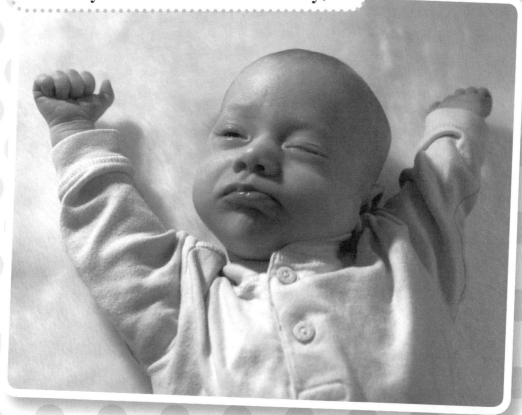

and that binge drinking is not
just for eighteen year olds,

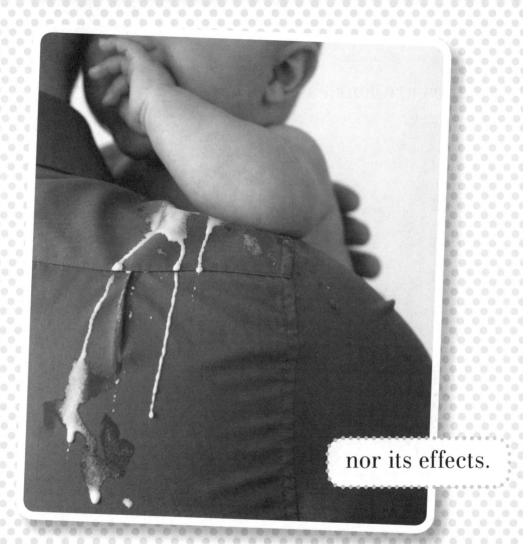

nor its effects.

Babies are fearless,

mischievous,

and more manipulative than a
contestant on *Survivor*.

They will make you
sick with worry,

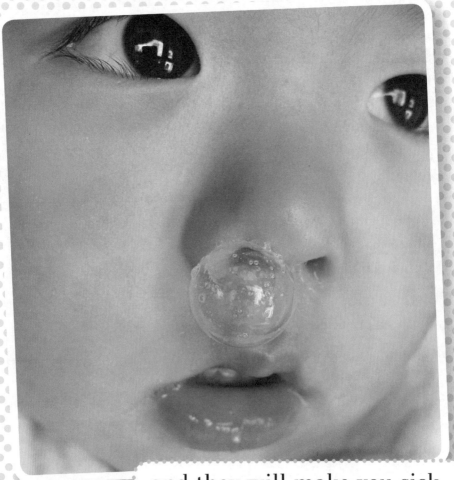

and they will make you sick.

They have a sound that
will break your heart,

and one that will
stop your heart.

Their skin puts a
silkworm to shame,

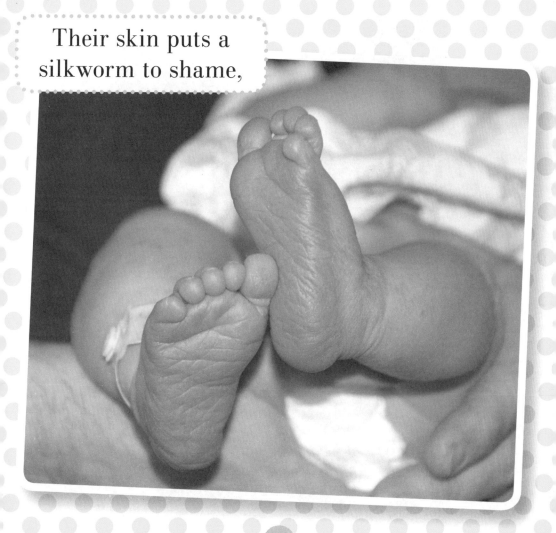

irresistible to
touch,

impossible not
to squeeze,

kiss,

or pinch.

A baby's smell is sweeter
than a morning bakery,

with just a hint of milk
past its 'use by' date.

Fingers and toes seem
too small to work,

but lungs are fully
functioning.

A baby can be a
performer one moment,

but often they just
need a moment.

Some can stand up
for themselves,

and some are
not so sure.

Sometimes a baby can look at you with a perception beyond their years,

an unnerving understanding
of the world around them,

and sometimes not.

A baby will make you
rethink 'quiet time',

the folly of repeating 'be gentle'
for the twentieth time,

and your own failings for not
making the world a better place,
instantly.

Sometimes babies will
find you boring.

They may not like
your singing,

or dancing.

Babies are not choosy about what they eat,

but they are choosy
about who they like.

Sharing a jumpsuit size does not make you instant friends,

but with one fart,
you are buddies for life.

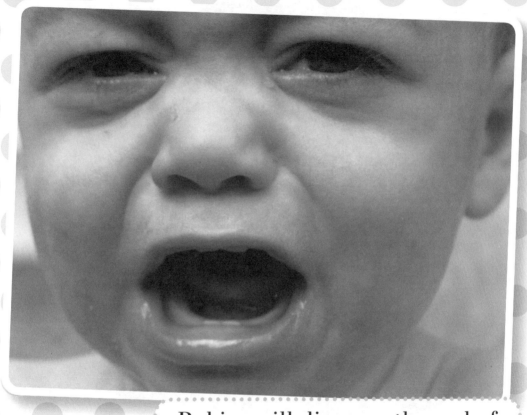

Babies will discover the end of
the world on an hourly basis,

that a button on the DVD remote
can make Snoopy speak Danish,

that every day holds
something new,

that privacy is a right
not yet earned,

or that life can all
get too much.

Babies believe some things
are worth sharing,

and some not.

A baby will not take
up much room,

but they will take
over every room.

No matter how much you fight it,
the tide of cuteness will be unstoppable.

Everywhere you look,
you will see something fluffy, squeaky . . .

. . . or unicorny.

You will be amazed by the number of strange guests that keep appearing.

Especially those freaky ones that
come to life in the night.

After conquering the house,
your car is next.

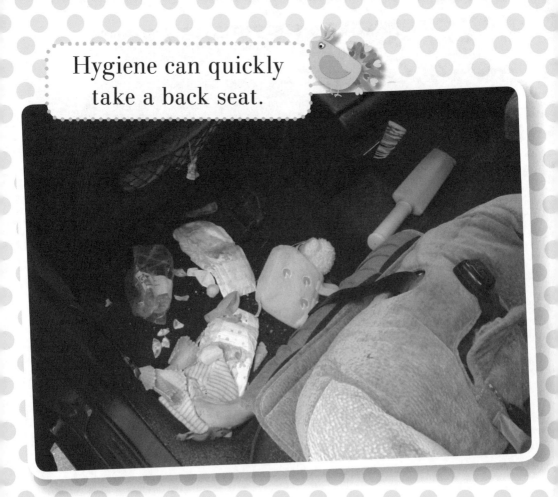

Hygiene can quickly take a back seat.

Pine scent will never replace these smells.
(The only answer is to replace the car.)

There is much to pack when you leave the house with a baby.

It helps to have two, or three, of everything

and god forbid if you
forget one of these.

You can watch a baby for hours:

a stretch will make
your heart skip,

a finished plate will make
your spirits soar,

just nothing will
be everything.

But try not to stare
too long.

Months are spent waiting for
your baby to crawl,

but within 24 hours you wish they would stop.

With all wheel drive, a baby
quickly heads off road,

up mountainous terrain,

but often makes time to monitor
road conditions,

or check under
the hood.

Babies discover the world by putting most of it in their mouth.

They will make you want to boil
furniture or disinfect a whole park.

Babies never remember the things
you can never forget:

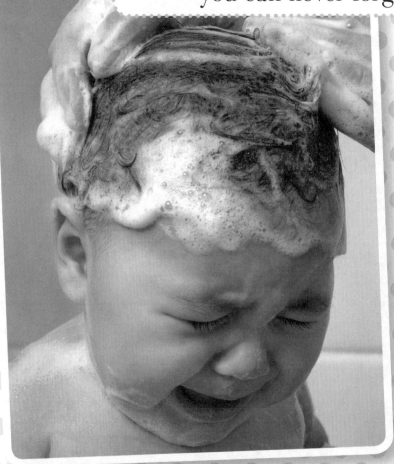

the uninvited arrival
of a tooth,

chafing that would bring a
marathon runner to tears,

a teenager's worst
nightmare,

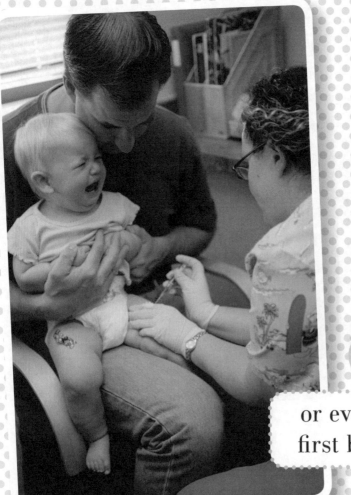

or even their
first betrayal.

But all will be
forgiven,

they will remain by your
side no matter what.

So even when they
wake the dead,

or the very dead,

when they scream 'I'm hungry',
'I'm in pain', 'I am in need of a change',

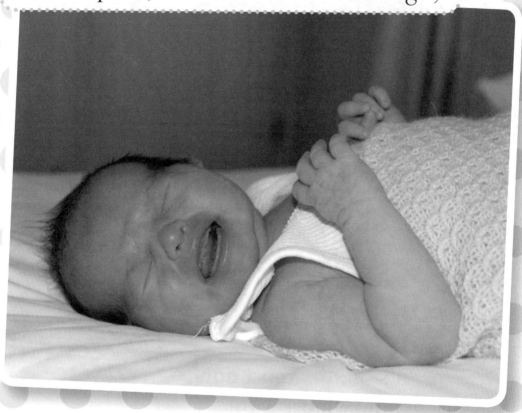

or 'it's 3 a.m. and I don't know what I want',

praise the world for
selective memory,

and always try to see
the funny side,

no matter what
comes up.

Picture credits